FUNNY
BUNNIES

FUNNY BUNNIES

Laurie Frankel

CHRONICLE BOOKS

SAN FRANCISCO

Text and photographs copyright
© 2004 by Laurie Frankel.

Library of Congress Cataloging-in-
Publication Data available.

ISBN 0-8118-4055-7

Manufactured in China

Design by Laurie Frankel
Bunny handling: Animal Arts
Backdrops by Kristie Oaks

Distributed in Canada by
Raincoast Books
9050 Shaughnessy Street
Vancouver, British Columbia V6P 6E5

10 9 8 7 6 5 4 3 2 1

Chronicle Books LLC
85 Second Street
San Francisco, California 94105

www.chroniclebooks.com

To my own little funny bunnies

"It doesn't happen all at once," said the Skin Horse. "You become. It takes a long time. That's why it doesn't happen often to people who break easily, or have sharp edges, or who have to be carefully kept. Generally, by the time you are Real, most of your hair has been loved off, and your eyes drop out and you get loose in your joints and very shabby. But these things don't matter at all, because once you are Real you can't be ugly, except to people who don't understand."

from The Velveteen Rabbit, by Margery Williams

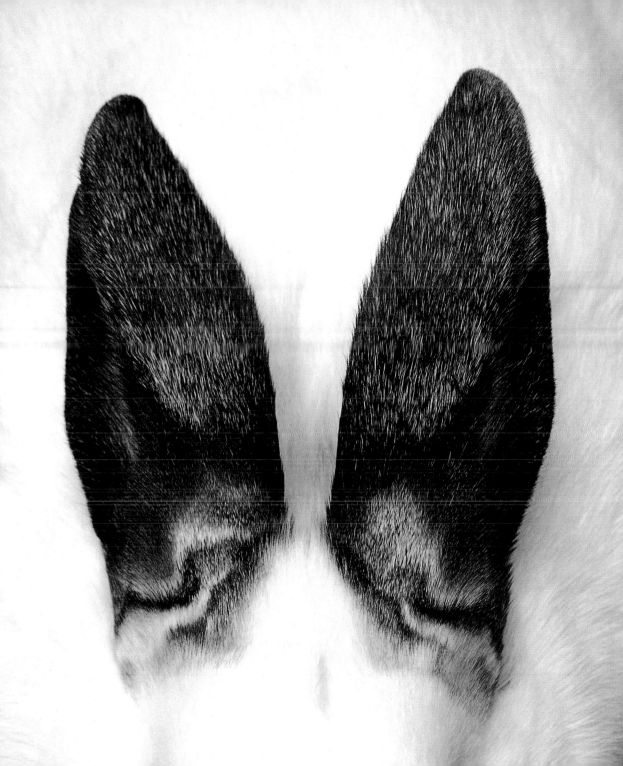

The quotation on the previous pages is the answer given to the Velveteen Rabbit when he asks how to become real. But it also says a lot about bunnies. To be real is to be loved. And bunnies, as everybody knows, are the most lovable of creatures.

Children especially love bunnies. The hands-down most popular person at my son's preschool was not a person at all but the school rabbit, Leo. All the kids vied for the privilege of feeding him, and when my husband and I came to visit, we were immediately introduced to him. It was as if, in Leo, the children had found their own perfect child to care for—trusting, gentle, and cute (and, of course, free of all the annoying traits of an actual little brother or sister).

I see bunny-love in adults, too. In pet stores and rabbit shows, I have spotted numerous grown-ups pausing before rabbit cages to wiggle their noses and nibble on pretend carrots.

My research for *Funny Bunnies* has given me a new understanding of rabbits. Not only have I learned about the amazing diversity of breeds, behaviors, and characteristics (did you know that rabbits digest their food twice?), I have also discovered the world of people dedicated to raising rabbits and spreading the word about the charm and warmth that bunnies can bring into a home.

I have heard story after story about how rabbits create joy. When I attended the American Rabbit Breeders Association convention, I was struck by how much the event resembled a giant family reunion, with the stories, the jokes, the tall tales. Though the family members might have different lifestyles—there were farmers, bikers, retirees, and young people—they all shared a "real" love for these sweet, quirky, and adorable funny bunnies.

Peter Rabbit, Peter Cottontail, Brer Rabbit, Uncle Wiggly, the March Hare, Thumper, Ski Bunnies, the Bunny Hop, the Year of the Rabbit, Honey Bunny, Honey Buns, Bunny Love. Rabbits have undeniably found their way into our culture and into our affections.

Who has grown up without patting the bunny in the classic children's book? Who has never been intrigued by the frenzied hurry of the White Rabbit in *Alice in Wonderland* or entertained by the devilish doings of Bugs Bunny? How would we appreciate Easter without the Easter Bunny and his basket of colored eggs, weird marshmallow chicks, and, best of all, chocolate replicas of him? The bunny may have many guises, but all of them reveal our fond feelings for the animal. Even our terms of endearment prominently feature bunnies.

So firmly is the bunny associated with cuteness and gentleness that it is surprising to learn of the rabbit's august stature in history. The hare was a symbol for the Greek goddess of love, Aphrodite, and was also linked with the Roman god Cupid. Even the Easter Bunny is an ancient creature, first celebrated by the Saxons some two thousand years ago to honor their goddess of spring and babies, Eastre. This goddess was so fond of rabbits that she turned her favorite bird into a bunny; to make up for the loss of its wings, she made the rabbit quick-on-its-feet and allowed it to lay eggs annually on the eve of her special day, the first full moon after the spring equinox. This is the foundation of our very own Easter Bunny, with his basket full of eggs painted to reflect the colors of spring.

In other cultures, the rabbit is also a symbol of good fortune, vigilance, and magical powers. Rabbits are often identified with the moon. In Egypt, for example, the hieroglyph for *hare* is also the symbol for the moon. In Chinese tradition, it is said that when you look at the moon, you will see a white rabbit mixing the elixir of immortality. Similarly, the rabbit appears on the moon in Buddhist mythology. According to one version of the story, Buddha disguised himself as a hungry old man and asked the animals to bring him food. All the animals offered up the carcasses of their prey, but the plant-eating rabbit, who had no prey, offered only himself. Greatly moved by the rabbit's self-sacrifice, Buddha placed the rabbit on the moon to shine as an example to all.

A sign of the Chinese zodiac, the rabbit in Eastern astrology symbolizes kindness, mercy, elegance, and devotion to beauty. Those who are born in the Year of the Rabbit are said to be kind, gentle of speech, peaceful, quiet, and loving.

In addition to these benign associations, rabbits are sometimes used as symbols of foolishness and guile. The term *hare-brained,* meaning senseless or crazy, is certainly uncomplimentary to hares and is derived from the erratic behavior of hares during their rutting season. The frivolous hare who loses an easy race to

the old tortoise in the folktale cautions against laziness and pride.

Perhaps one of the reasons rabbits and hares have been the stuff of legend for so long is that there are so many of them! Rabbits lived in Asia as long as 65 million years ago, and in North America 35 million years ago. They are extremely adaptable and live in an amazing variety of habitats, including arid deserts, flat grasslands, alpine valleys, tropical rain forests, and even in the cold, snowy arctic. In fact, rabbits and hares can be found in just about every climate and country in the world.

Rabbits and hares are both lagomorphs, that is, a gnawing herbivorous mammal with two pairs of incisors. Though rabbits and hares look similar, they are actually different species. Hares are larger, and their hind legs and their ears are longer than those of rabbits. Additionally, baby hares, also known as leverettes, are born with a full coat of fur and their eyes wide open. In contrast, baby rabbits are born with their eyes closed, hairless, and helpless. Rabbits are very social creatures, living in large communities, or warrens, of up to one hundred rabbits,

whereas hares prefer to live by themselves until mating time.

Domestic rabbits belong to a single species, descended from the European rabbit, *Oryctolagus cuniculus*, which rather unpoetically translates as "hare-like digger of underground passages." There are now many breeds of domestic rabbits ranging in size from bunnies as small as the two-pound Netherland Dwarf to the aptly named Flemish Giant, which may grow to be eighteen or nineteen pounds. Bunnies come in all kinds of colors, from white to black to speckled, deckled, chestnut, and more. A rabbit's fur length and texture also vary from breed to breed: some rabbits have very short hair, while others have long silky hair. The long fur of the Angora rabbit, which can grow over an inch a month, is used like wool to make cozy mittens and sweaters. Each breed of rabbit, as you will see, has its own distinctive characteristics.

Of course, the most famous attribute of the rabbit is its ears. In addition to being very cute, ears help regulate a rabbit's temperature. Rabbit ears usually range from two to four inches, although the English Lop has ears that can measure up to twelve inches long. Rabbits also have keen vision and, as everybody knows, very big teeth! A rabbit's eyes are eight times more sensitive to light than are ours, and its teeth grow continuously throughout its life. In fact, the only reason that rabbits' teeth don't grow halfway down their chins is that they are constantly being ground down by incessant chewing. Rabbits prefer crunchy foods like carrots and celery for this reason—to keep those incisors well filed.

Rabbits are most active at dawn and dusk, when they like to eat and play. They sleep during the day. When happy, rabbits will perform a series of jumps, twists, runs, or combinations of these; the term for these antics is *binky*. It is very important to distinguish these behaviors from the rabbit warning signal, called thumping, which occurs when rabbits pound their back legs against the floor or ground. When you see a rabbit thump, watch out! Rabbits thump when they are anxious or stressed or when they want something, like food.

Rabbits have a scent gland under their chin. When you see a rabbit rubbing its chin, it is leaving its scent (odorless to us) to mark territory, or chinning. Rabbits also make a variety of unique sounds to communicate. Like a dog, a bunny will growl if it is mad. Males purr when they are feeling romantic.

Funny Bunnies is a collection of thirty breeds and their characteristics. If this book inspires you to get a pet rabbit, please read up on the particular breed before you bring one home. Bunnies make great pets (they can even be trained to use a litter box!), but like all pets, they have their quirks, and each requires special care and attention. The Recommended Reading list (page 94) and the Bunny Organizations section (pages 92–93) provide information you need to research the kind of bunny that is best for you and learn about its proper care. One final note of caution for those who are seeking a pet: with rabbits, smaller is not necessarily better. Netherland Dwarfs, so adorable because they can fit in the palm of your hand, may actually be quite nasty. The larger breeds are often gentler and therefore preferable as pets.

But *Funny Bunnies* isn't just a guide to selecting a pet. It's a catalog of cuteness and—for me, anyway—an unfailing mood enhancer. There's nothing like a bunny to make you feel better after a bad day, and if you can't have one nestled in your lap, then looking at *Funny Bunnies* will be the next best thing.

COLORS:
black
black tortoiseshell
blue
blue-eyed white
blue tortoiseshell
broken pattern
chestnut
chinchilla
chocolate
fawn
lilac
lynx
opal
orange
pointed white
ruby-eyed white
sable point
Siamese sable
Siamese smoke pearl
squirrel

horace

ORIGIN: United States (New York) | WEIGHT: approximately 3 lbs

The American Fuzzy Lop is a short and, well, fuzzy rabbit that comes in twenty different colors. It is a fairly new breed developed from the Holland Lop and Angora rabbits.

With droopy ears that extend approximately a half to one inch below the jaw, the American Fuzzy Lop is a relatively short rabbit known for its sweet disposition. Horace is especially sweet when he gets a peanut butter sandwich. Lops of all kinds are among the most popular rabbits with breeders as well as pet owners.

BREED: **BELGIAN HARE**

COLOR:
reddish chestnut

Despite their name, Belgian Hares are not really hares, nor are they from Belgium. Belgian Hares are really English rabbits, and they are called hares because they are as agile as hares.

The slender, lithe Belgian Hare is a particularly elegant rabbit, sporting long, straight ears; dense, short hair; and hazel eyes. It is also one of the most intelligent breeds. Not only can it be housebroken, but it can also learn to obey commands. At rabbit exhibitions Belgian Hares have been known to change their pose in response to their trainer's whistle. For those whose rabbits compete on the showtable, a considerable amount of time is spent teaching them to sit tall.

jefferson

ORIGIN: England   WEIGHT: **6** to **9** lbs

harvey

ORIGIN: Belgium | **WEIGHT:** **8** to **12** lbs

Beverens originated in Beveren, Belgium, in the late nineteenth century, but they became popular in England in the twentieth. The first Beverens were blue, though unlike other blue rabbits, their coats are actually a shade of lavender. The white Beveren is currently in great demand, for, unlike most white rabbits, the white Beveren has blue eyes.

COLOR:

champagne

agnes

ORIGIN: France WEIGHT: **9** to **11** lbs

The French Argent, or Champagne d'Argent, rabbit is one of France's oldest breeds of fancy rabbits. They are born black and acquire a silvered effect as they age, usually beginning to show adult coloring from two to four months. They were given their moniker because of the region of France where they were first developed. (Crème d'Argents, a more recent breed, are born orange and develop white ticking within the same time period.)

Champagnes are a cross of the St. Nicholas Giant and the Vienna Blue.

COLOR:

white with red
eyes and black
nose, ears, feet,
and tail

spiro

ORIGIN: United States (California)	WEIGHT: **8** to **10** lbs

As the name indicates, the Californian was first bred in California from a mix of New Zealand White, Himalayan, and Standard Chinchilla rabbits. The Californian is known among rabbit fanciers as an all-purpose rabbit, which means that they make fine pets.

Spiro entertains herself by hopping wildly around the house whenever she hears music.

CHINCHILLA GIANT

COLOR:

gray with black
and white ticking

attila

ORIGIN: France   **WEIGHT:** **12** to **16** lbs

One of the biggest bunnies, the Chinchilla Giant, a larger version of the Chinchilla, is known for its kindly temperament and fairly slow gait. As with most of the larger female rabbits, or does, Giant Chinchilla does have a dewlap (an extra roll of skin and fur under the chin), which makes them look quite dignified. It is from this area that the does pull fur for their nests.

Attila was named after Attila the Hun, but she hasn't lived up to her name. She's very gentle and sweet and would never invade a country. Here she is with her good friend Lilo, a Netherland Dwarf.

BREED: **DUTCH**

COLORS:

black

blue

chocolate

gray

steel

tortoiseshell

checks & mate

ORIGIN: **Netherlands** | WEIGHT: $3\frac{1}{2}$ to $5\frac{1}{2}$ lbs

These cute little rabbits make wonderful pets for children, for they are gentle, good-natured, and look just like Peter Rabbit. The colorful markings on their bottoms make them look as if they were wearing trousers, and, in fact, they are sometimes known as the Tuxedo Breed. One of the interesting characteristics of the Dutch rabbit is that the females will adopt the offspring of others and care for them as if they were their own.

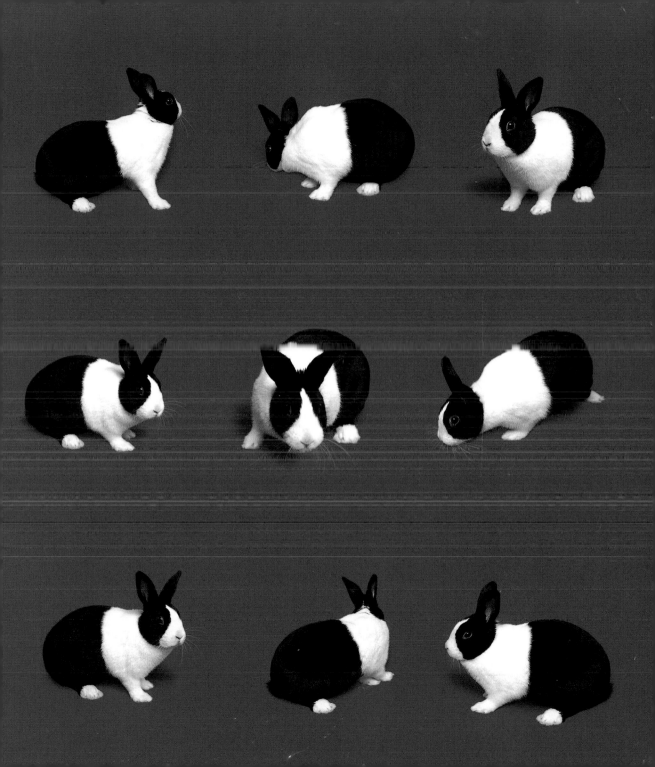

BREED: DWARF HOTOT

COLOR:

white

shirley, ruth & selma

ORIGIN: Germany | WEIGHT: **2** to **3** lbs

With its white fur and band of black around its dark brown eyes, this tiny rabbit is sometimes referred to as the mascara bunny. First bred in Germany, the Hotot (pronounced ho-tow) is lovable and curious, but as you can see here, these rabbits can become very moody if they're ignored.

BREED: **ENGLISH ANGORA**

COLORS:

black

blue

blue-eyed white

blue steel

blue tortoiseshell

chestnut

chocolate

chocolate chestnut

chocolate chinchilla

chocolate steel

chocolate tortoiseshell

chinchilla

copper

cream

fawn

lilac

lilac chinchilla

lilac steel

lilac tortoiseshell

lynx

opal

pearl

pointed white

red

ruby-eyed white

sable

seal

smoke pearl

squirrel

steel

tortoiseshell

tribble

ORIGIN: Turkey, then England | WEIGHT: **5** to **7** lbs

Yes, you can pull a rabbit out from under all that hair. The Angora is the only rabbit whose fur is so long that it can be used for spinning. The fur may be plucked (which is not in the least painful) from the rabbit, or shorn. The yarn made from the fur is warmer than sheep's wool and provides warmth without much weight. The English Angora is among the smallest of the Angora breeds.

Tribble is so affectionate that he gives kisses to his family each morning. He loves attention, even from the dog, and seems to be under the impression that humans are helpless creatures that he has generously allowed to live in his home.

41

COLORS:

blue

chocolate

gold

gray

lilac

tortoiseshell

white with black

sparky

ORIGIN: England | **WEIGHT: 5 to 8 lbs**

The English Spot has the exact same markings on each side, a butterfly marking across the nose and lips, a little beauty mark on each cheek, with a spotted stripe down the back. The breed was developed from the interestingly named Butterfly Smut rabbit.

Sparky is a daredevil. He likes racing and will chase the mail carrier when he gets a chance.

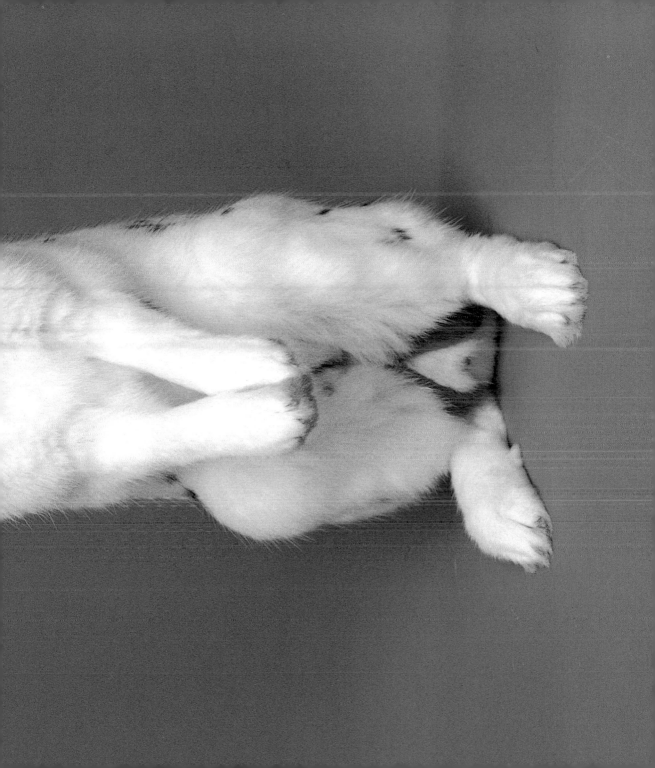

BREED: **ENGLISH LOP**

COLORS:

black	brokens	frosted black	lynx	silver
black chinchilla	chinchilla	frosted blue	opal	silver fox
black steel	chestnut	frosted chocolate	orange	smoke pearl
black tortoiseshell	chocolate	frosted lilac	red	smoke pearl chinchilla
blue	chocolate chinchilla	frosted pearl	red-eyed white	steel
blue chinchilla	chocolate steel	lilac	sable	tri-colored
blue-eyed white	chocolate tortoiseshell	lilac chinchilla	sable chinchilla	tortoiseshell
blue steel	cream	lilac steel	sable point	
blue tortoiseshell		lilac tortoiseshell	seal	

dumbo

ORIGIN: Africa   WEIGHT: **9** lbs

Researchers have found that the English Lop breed existed as far back as the mid-1700s, making it the oldest known breed of domestic rabbit. It is certainly one of the most flamboyant, for its ears are the longest of all rabbits, measuring up to twelve inches in length. The English Lop is so prized by rabbit breeders that it is sometimes called "the King of the Fancy." However, the English Lop's dashing appearance is often coupled with a rather erratic temperament. English Lops have been known to chew at their ears when they are frightened or stressed (the ears do not grow back). Other lops include the Holland Lop, Mini Lop, and French Lop.

Dumbo is constantly tripping over his ears, and we doubt he will ever get used to them!

COLORS:

black

blue

fawn

light gray

sandy

steel

flausious

ORIGIN: **Flanders** WEIGHT: **14** to **20** lbs

The Flemish Giant is the largest breed of rabbit. These bunnies usually weigh in at about fifteen pounds, but it's not unusual to see a twenty pound Flemish Giant. Its ears, which stand up straight, may be six and a half inches, and its short hair is often gray or sandy red. They make excellent pets: like dogs, they are loyal and devoted, and like cats, they like to snooze in the sun.

Flausious is one of the more cat-like Flemish Giants. He loves flowers and spends his days relaxing in his own garden.

BREED: **FRENCH ANGORA**

COLORS:

blue-eyed white

blue steel

chestnut

chinchilla

cinnamon

chocolate chinchilla

chocolate steel

chocolate tortoiseshell

copper

cream

dark sable

fawn

frosted pearl

lilac cream

lilac chinchilla

lilac steel

lynx

opal

pointed white

red

ruby-eyed white

sable

smoked pearl

squirrel

steel

tortoiseshell

wild gray

licorice

ORIGIN: France	WEIGHT: **7** to **10** lbs

Developed by the French for its wool, the French Angora has a wooly body and short hair around the ears, face, and feet. A high percentage of guard hair in their coats makes them easier to maintain than some of the other Angoras.

Rabbits are meticulous groomers, and very much like cats, are prone to hairballs. Unlike cats, they cannot regurgitate, so wool breeds are susceptible to intestinal blockage that can be fatal. Papaya pills or fresh papaya are common and effective as preventive measures.

romulus & remus

ORIGIN: France & England | **WEIGHT: 10 to 12 lbs**

Though the French Lop's ears are long, they are considerably shorter than those of the English Lop. The French Lop rabbit was first bred in France around 1850, a cross between the English Lop and the Butterfly rabbit of France.

Romulus somehow intuits his Butterfly rabbit origin, and, using his long ears as wings, leaps forward and attempts to fly.

BREED: **HAVANA**

COLORS:

black

blue

chocolate

kronos

ORIGIN: Netherlands   WEIGHT: **4** to **6** lbs

The Havana is a short, round rabbit with erect ears set close together. It was first discovered in a Dutch rabbit's litter in Holland in 1898, although no one knew the breed of the buck. The chocolate Havana's fur often looks purplish, and its eyes have the peculiar property of glowing red in the dark, though they are brown by sunlight.

Kronos is a very docile bunny and likes to snuggle up to whoever comes near.

twiggy

ORIGIN: France | **WEIGHT: 8 to 11 lbs**

Also known as Blanc de Hotot, a larger version of the Dwarf Hotot, the Hotot is white except for the dramatic black circles around the eyes, which make it look like a 1920s movie star.

As is fitting for a movie star, Twiggy can't stop talking about herself. She chatters all day long, even when she's eating.

BREED: **JERSEY WOOLY**

COLORS:

black	opal
black otter	pointed white
blue	ruby-eyed white
blue-eyed white	sable marten
blue otter	sable point
blue tortoiseshell	seal
chestnut	silver marten
chinchilla	siamese sable
chocolate	smoke pearl
lilac	squirrel
marten	tortoiseshell

bruce

ORIGIN: United States (New Jersey)

WEIGHT: under 3 lbs

The Jersey Wooly gets its name from its birth state, New Jersey. One of the smallest of the breeds, the Jersey Wooly usually stays under three pounds.

Bruce's family made a stage for him, and he loves to perform. He skitters back and forth all day, because apparently he likes the sound his toenails make on the wood.

BREED: **LILAC**

COLOR:

lilac

ORIGIN: **England**   WEIGHT: **5½** to **8** lbs

Lilac rabbits are a cross between a Havana and a Blue Beveren and were originally known as the Cambridge Blue. Lilac rabbits have a silky, beautiful coat, and their eyes match their fur, which is best described as a pink-tinted dove gray.

Eyore loves to eat Cheerios and sunflower seeds, but he gets lots of crumbs and bits in his fur, which makes him look like a crazy old man.

nala

ORIGIN: Belgium   **WEIGHT: $3\frac{1}{2}$ lbs**

Lion Heads, or "Têtes de Lion," as they are called in France, originated from the miniature Swiss Fox, the Belgian Dwarf, and possibly the Jersey Wooly as well. There were no lions involved, but the result was a ruff around the head similar to the mane of a lion. Despite the resemblance, Lion Heads are not at all fierce. They are excellent mothers and will pull their own fur out to make their babies' nests more comfortable.

Nala, for example, is the proud mother of thirty little Lion Heads and plans to give them many more siblings.

BREED: **MINI LOP**

COLORS:

fifty different varieties,
including all the broken
and tricolor combinations

ginger

ORIGIN: **Germany** | WEIGHT: **4½** to **6** lbs

Mini Lops, also known as German Lops, have become very popular in the past few years, probably because they are so cute and lively. The Miniature Lop was developed from the French Lop, the Netherland Dwarf, and possibly the Chinchilla as well. Even though these bunnies are very small, they are quite muscular. They need a lot of daily exercise, and some even like to be walked on a leash.

Ginger is a great gymnast. Once she jumped for over five hours straight (but she had to sleep for a long time afterward).

BREED: **MINI REX**

COLORS:

black

blue

broken pattern

castor chinchilla

chocolate

Himalayan

lilac

lynx

opal

red

seal

tortoiseshell

white

jack, zack, mack, hack & flack

ORIGIN: **United States (Texas)** | WEIGHT: **3** to **4½** lbs

In general, Rex rabbits come in two sizes, standard and mini. Known as the "original velveteen rabbit" because of its wonderful plush velvety fur, the Rex has more under-fur than most other rabbits, making it irresistibly cuddly. Both the Standard and Mini Rex may have multiple color variations, and breeders are continually trying to develop new colors.

These siblings love playing together and especially doing the bunny hop.

COLORS

Available in
several colors
including red,
black, and white

sport

ORIGIN: New Zealand & Germany | WEIGHT: **6** to **10** lbs

Sport is an interesting mixture of a commercial breed (New Zealand, originally brought to the United States from New Zealand by sailors who perhaps intended to eat them), and the very popular fancy breed, Mini Lop.

Sport's parents must have made an unusual couple with his father averaging ten pounds, and his mother only 6 lbs; however, both New Zealands and Mini Lops make excellent pets with docile temperaments.

When Sport is not terrorizing the cat, she loves to be draped over a shoulder and carried around the house.

BREED: **MIXED**
HIMALAYAN AND CALIFORNIA

COLORS:

white with
blue, black, or
chocolate
markings

mika

ORIGIN: Himalayas and United States WEIGHT: **2** to **4** lbs

If Mika showed more of her Himalayan daddy, she would have shorter ears and a long cylindrical body. Like her daddy, her nose, ears, feet, and tail are cooler than the rest of her body, a genetically transmitted trait.

This breed of rabbit gets her name from her natural habitat north and south of the Himalayans, but he is also known as the Russian, Chinese, Egyptian, and the Black Nose. The Himalayan's nose, feet, tail, and ears can be black or blue, but the rest of the body is always white with pink eyes.

Mika wouldn't have won any shows for representing the perfect Himalayan, but she sure is cute and cuddly!

BREED: **NETHERLAND DWARF**

COLORS:

black	fawn	ruby-eyed white	smoke pearl
blue	Himalayan	sable marten	smoke pearl marten
blue-eyed white	lilac	sable point	squirrel
chestnut chinchilla	lynx	Siamese sable	steel
chocolate	opal	silver marten	tan
	orange		tortoiseshell
	otter		

dexter, euclid, hector & robin

ORIGIN: Netherlands | **WEIGHT:** **1** to **2½** lbs

Netherland Dwarfs are the smallest breed of rabbit, fitting nicely into the palm of your hand or—watch out!—your shoe. But they can be very touchy, so it's best to treat them with respect. They come in a rainbow of rabbit colors and have round heads and short, erect ears.

As you can see, one of these siblings is very shy and one is feisty (we think it's due to a Napoleon complex). They argue all day long.

BREED: **POLISH**

COLORS:

black

blue

blue-eyed white

broken

chocolate

ruby-eyed white

khan

ORIGIN: England & Germany | WEIGHT: under **3½** lbs

The Polish rabbit is sometimes confused with the Netherland Dwarf, since they both are small bunnies. However, the Polish's ears are usually about an inch longer than those of the Netherland Dwarf, and its face is not as round. Like the Netherland Dwarf, the Polish is a rather crabby bunny and is best left to itself. A Polish rabbit will not tolerate sharing its hutch with another rabbit, and if such a thing is attempted, vicious fighting will ensue.

Khan is a fearsome bunny. That's what he thinks, anyway.

opie

ORIGIN: France | **WEIGHT:** 7½ to 10 lbs

Like the Mini Rex, the Standard Rex is
known for its soft, plush coat, which made
it much prized among rabbit fanciers
when it was introduced at the beginning
of the twentieth century. One of the first
proponents of the Rex rabbit was King
Albert of Belgium, and though the breed
was unknown at rabbit exhibitions, the
judges were loath to refuse their king an
opportunity to display his treasured rabbits. Accordingly, they showed them with
the label Rex, to indicate that they
belonged to the king, and the name stuck.
The Standard Rex, now no longer a rarity,
is bred in a plethora of colors.

Unaware of his royal lineage, Opie loves
bananas and is willing to jump for them.
He sticks his head out when he wants to
be petted.

BREED: **STANDARD REX**

COLORS:

black

black otter

blue

broken

Californian

castor

chinchilla

chocolate

lilac

lynx

opal

red

sable

seal

white

BREED: SATIN

COLORS:

black

blue

broken (white with a
   pattern of black,
   blue, chocolate,
   copper or red)

Californian

chinchilla

chocolate

copper

otter

red

ruby-eyed white

Siamese

chelsea

ORIGIN: United States (Indiana) | **WEIGHT: 8 to 11 lbs**

Satins were clearly named for their lustrous coats, which seem to shimmer like satin. They look as though they are dressed for a ball. Satins come in a number of colors. An all-time favorite is the Siamese, which has the same coloring as the cat by that name.

Chelsea is quite a flirt and is obviously very proud of her fancy fur.

BREED: **SILVER MARTEN**

COLORS:

black

blue

chocolate

sable with silver-tipped
 guard hairs

cecile

ORIGIN: **United States**   WEIGHT: **6** to **9½** lbs

The Silver Marten, which was developed from the Chinchilla, has perhaps the most dramatic markings of any rabbit: white-rimmed eyes, ears, nose, and chin against dark fur. With white paws, underside, tail, and neck triangle and a frost of white ticking up their sides, these are especially distinguished bunnies.

Cecile pretends to be shy, but if you play the harmonica, she'll wiggle and twist and dance.

BUNNY ORGANIZATIONS

**AMERICAN BEVEREN
RABBIT CLUB**
P.O. Box 65
Sunfield, MI 48890

**AMERICAN BLUE AND
WHITE RABBIT CLUB**
255 East Line Rd.
Ballston Lake, NY 12019

**AMERICAN BRITTANNIA
PETITE RABBIT SOCIETY**
4092 King Dr.
West Richland, WA
99353-9331

**AMERICAN CHINCHILLA
RABBIT BREEDERS
ASSOCIATION**
1017 S. Hillcrest
Springfield, MO 65802-5113

**AMERICAN DUTCH RABBIT
CLUB, INC.**
Rt. 1 Box 95
Lewiston, MN 55952

**AMERICAN DWARF HOTOT
RABBIT CLUB**
4061 Tremont Ave.
Egg Harbor Township, NJ 08234-9421

**AMERICAN ENGLISH SPOT
RABBIT CLUB**
513 E. Kent St.
Lubbock, TX 79403-1609

**AMERICAN FEDERATION OF
NEW ZEALAND RABBIT
BREEDERS**
23628 S. Hwy 211
Colton, OR 97017

**AMERICAN FUZZY LOP
RABBIT CLUB**
14255 S.E. Stephens
Portland, OR 97233

**AMERICAN NETHERLAND
DWARF RABBIT CLUB**
326 Travis Ln.
Rockwall, TX 75032

**AMERICAN POLISH RABBIT
CLUB**
417 Washington Ave.
Terrace Park, OH 45174

**AMERICAN RABBIT
BREEDERS ASSOCIATION
(ARBA)**
P.O. Box 426
Bloomington, IL 61702
www.arba.net

**AMERICAN SABLE RABBIT
SOCIETY**
3360 Graham Rd.
Rising Sun, OH 43457

**AMERICAN SATIN RABBIT
BREEDERS ASSOCIATION**
316 South Mahaffie
Olathe, KS 66061

**AMERICAN STANDARD
CHINCHILLA RABBIT
ASSOCIATION**
7905 Thompson Twp. Rd. 81
Bellevue, OH 44811

**CALIFORNIAN RABBIT
SPECIALTY CLUB**
22162 S. Hunter Rd.
Colton, OR 97017

**CHAMPAGNE D'ARGENT
RABBIT FEDERATION**
1704 Heisel Ave.
Pekin, IL 61554

**CRÈME D'ARGENT RABBIT
FEDERATION**
2293 Factory Rd.
Albany, OH 45710

GIANT CHINCHILLA RABBIT
FEDERATION
2019 Co Rd. 137
Cardington, OH 43315

HAVANA RABBIT BREEDERS
ASSOCIATION
P.O. Drawer O
Cortez, CO 81321

HOLLAND LOP RABBIT
SPECIALTY CLUB
2633 Seven Eleven Rd.
Chesapeake, VA 23322

HOTOT RABBIT BREEDERS
INTERNATIONAL
583 Bonita Dr.
Blanco, TX 78606

HOUSE RABBIT SOCIETY
1524 Benton St.
Alameda, CA 94501
www.rabbit.org

LOP RABBIT CLUB OF
AMERICA
P.O. Box 8367
Fremont, CA 94537-8367

MINI LOP RABBIT CLUB OF
AMERICA
P.O. Box 17
Pittsburgh, KS 66762

NATIONAL ANGORA RABBIT
BREEDERS CLUB
2380 Co. Rd. 9 NE
Nelson, MN 56355

NATIONAL FEDERATION OF
FLEMISH GIANT RABBIT
BREEDERS
2259 Barbara Dr.
Camarillo, CA 93012

NATIONAL JERSEY WOOLY
RABBIT CLUB
1311 Poe Ln.
San Jose, CA 95130

NATIONAL LILAC RABBIT
CLUB OF AMERICA
9502 Richmond Rd.
Belding, MI 48809

NATIONAL MINI REX
RABBIT CLUB
1105 20th Ave.
Pipestone, MN 56164

NATIONAL REX RABBIT
CLUB
21840 S. 116th Ave.
New Lenox, IL 60451

NATIONAL SILVER RABBIT
CLUB
1030 S.W. KK Hwy.
Holden, MO 64040-8221

RABBITS ONLY
P.O. Box 207
Holbrook, NY 11741
www.rabbits.com

RHINELANDER RABBIT
CLUB OF AMERICA
1560 Vine St.
El Centro, CA 92243

SILVER MARTEN RABBIT
CLUB
2113 Sommer St.
Napa, CA 94559

INDEX

RECOMMENDED READING:

American Rabbit Breeders Association. *Standard of Perfection.* Bloomington, IL: American Rabbit Breeders Association Publications, 2001.

Brown, Margaret Wise. *The Runaway Bunny,* illustrated by Clement Hurd. New York: HarperCollins Children's Books, 1972.

Carroll, Lewis. *Alice's Adventures in Wonderland.* Oxford, UK: Clarendon Press, 1865.

Gendron, Karen. *The Rabbit Handbook.* New York: Barron's Educational Series, 2000.

Harriman, Marinell. *House Rabbit Handbook, 3d ed.* Alameda, CA: Drollery Press, 1995.

Heyward, Du Bose. *The Country Bunny.* Boston and New York: Houghton Mifflin, 1939.

Hunter, Samantha and Samantha Fraser. *Hop to It: A Guide to Training Your Pet Rabbit.* New York: Barrons Educational Series, 1991.

McBride, Anne. *Why Does My Rabbit...?* London: Souvenir Press, 1999.

Potter, Beatrix. *Beatrix Potter: The Complete Tales.* London: Peter Rabbit Books, 2002.

Rabbits Only magazine. P.O. Box 207, Holbrook, New York 11741.

Robinson, David. *Encyclopedia of Pet Rabbits.* Neptune City, NJ: T.F.H. Publications, 1979.

Siino, Betsy Sikora. *The Essential Rabbit.* Hoboken, NJ: Wiley, 1998.

Taylor, David. *Rabbit Handbook.* New York: Sterling, 1999

Williams, Margery. *The Velveteen Rabbit.* New York: Doubleday, 1958.

ACKNOWLEDGMENTS

I would like to thank Leslie Jonath for her vision of *Funny Bunnies* and for bringing it to life. Her ideas, enthusiasm, energy, and talent—not to mention all of her time—have made it come together. Her encouragement always makes me want to push way beyond the edge.

Thank you to Brett MacFadden for his inspiration, creativity, and direction. Thanks also to Annie Barrows, Lisa Campbell, Tera Killip, Jan Hughes, Laurel Mainard, Doug Ogan, and Michelle Thomas.

I am very grateful to Tonna and Tex Thomas, for all their expertise, and to Danielle Hayduk, for hers.

Special thanks to our studio managers, Caitlin Parker and Courtney L. Pease. And to Barbara and Grace Gesswein and Grand Champion Software for being such wonderful roommates.

A giant thank you to the many, many wonderful people at the Peoria American Rabbit Breeders Association convention. Everyone was so incredibly helpful, genuine, and open that they made our team feel right at home. An extra-special thanks to Norma Hart and to Richard Gehr, co-chairs of the seventy-ninth ARBA Convention, for making it all come together so quickly.

Hugs to my honey bunny, Gary, and to my very own funny bunnies, Xander and Julius, who guided me toward the cutest and funniest bunnies and who put up with me at the many county and state fairs. And finally, thanks to Erin Korff; Kate Kunath; Animal Arts; Jill, Carly, and Olivia Ray; Carol Manos; Nancy Hinkston; Kristie Oaks; Tracy Astle; and Jenny Heath for all their help.

My appreciation and thanks to all the owners of the lovely bunnies I photographed:

Bertha Ainsworth

Charla Allen

Criss Bicling

Victor Bloom

Wendy Brabender

Connie Burant

Nora & Michael Burkhard

DeeAnn & Wade Burkhalter

Peggy Campbell

Sean Carrigan

Cara & Erica Dannemiller

Steve Dehn

Erin & Jacqueline Drozinski

Marian Eley

Debbie Ernst

Dawson Funk

Liz & Jennie Gates

Barbara & Grace Gesswein

Nicole Gibeault

Catherine A. Greig

Brian Hartzell

Elaine Harvey

Mark Jacobs

Randy Kummer

Melba Lackey

John M. Lindh

Peggy Luers

Cheryl Miller

Vern Miller

John Mlindh

Deborah Owens

Anthony & Crystal Parker

Courtney L. Pease

Christy Pratt

Marcus Rhoden

Dana & Denise Roberts

Irene Sanchez

Miranda Sanchez

Terry Stricker

David & Lorelei Szatkowski

Donna Towell

Suzanne Treudt

Mary Walton

Lori Whitson

Scott Wiebensohn

Peggy Wuers